Johann Sebastian Bach

Hero of Faith

By Barry L. Bobb

Illustrated by Linda Pierce

CONCORDIA PUBLISHING HOUSE • SAINT LOUIS

Copyright © 2011 Concordia Publishing House
3558 S. Jefferson Ave., St. Louis, MO 63118-3968
1-800-325-3040 • www.cph.org

Written by Barry L. Bobb
Illustrated by Linda Pierce
Edited by Rodney L. Rathmann
Editorial assistant: Amanda G. Lansche

Manufactured in Burlington, WI / 034280 / 160011

For Phyllis and Richard Duesenberg,
*who have done so much to bring the genius
and joy of Bach to others*

*Special thanks to the following for their careful
reading of the manuscript and helpful comments:*
Donna Bobb, Jean Darling, Mark Bender,
Marshall and Zack Murphy

Table of Contents

When long before time and the worlds were begun,

when there was no earth and no sky and no sun,

and all was deep silence and night reigned supreme,

and even our Maker had only a dream—

The silence was broken when God sang the Song,

and light pierced the darkness and rhythm began,

and with its first birth-cries creation was born,

and creaturely voices sang praise to the morn.

The sounds of the creatures were one with their Lord's,

their harmonies sweet and befitting the Word;

the Singer was pleased as the earth sang the Song,

the choir of the creatures re-echoed it long.

Though down through the ages the Song disappeared,

its harmonies broken and almost unheard,

the Singer comes to us to sing it again,

our God-is-with-us in the world now as then.

hero of
faith

◆ ◆ ◆

chapter one
Sebastian Is Born

Thuringia, a region in central Germany (1685)

Imagine a time and a place very different from our own. It is March 1685. In a valley between rolling hills is the small town of Eisenach. It lies in the countryside in Thuringia, a region in central Germany. Forests of ancient fir trees cover the hillsides, and farm animals graze in green pastures. Old wooden fences crisscross the landscape. It is early spring, and streams flow down the hills and line the valley as flowers begin to bloom.

High on a hilltop, the great Wartburg castle towers over the small homes of Eisenach. In the town below, people walk past the large church and through the busy marketplace. Eisenach is full of many different sounds as friends stop to chat, mothers shop, and children play in the crowded streets. Even from a distance, you can hear the conversations mix together as people walk around.

In a time before radio, video games, the Internet, and cable TV, music seems to be *everywhere*. Most people sing and play instruments.

Families make music together in their homes, and worshipers sing hymns loudly in church. People even sing in the streets, entertaining anyone who will listen. This is a beautiful, enchanted place— the kind of place where great moments in history can happen.

Music seems to be everywhere.

*Over 150 years earlier, the Wartburg castle
was the hideout for the great reformer Martin Luther.*

Over 150 years earlier, the Wartburg castle
was the hideout for the great reformer Martin
Luther. His efforts to reform the Church had
made him many enemies. In fact, the emperor
had proclaimed him an outlaw and placed him
on the government's "most wanted" list! When a
price was put on Luther's head, his prince, Frederick of Saxony (also known as Frederick the Wise),
had his soldiers pretend to capture Luther and
bring him to this great castle for his own pro-
tection. Luther would later remember how safe
he felt in this place when he wrote the song
"A Mighty Fortress Is Our God." Martin Luther
could not have known that many years later

another important person—some would say the greatest musician in the history of the world—would be born here, in Eisenach.

March 21 arrives, the first day of spring and a time of new life. Another baby is born to the large family of Ambrosius and Mary Elizabeth Bach—the youngest of ten brothers and sisters. They name him Johann Sebastian, but everyone calls him Sebastian. After a few days, his parents bring him to the church to be baptized, and God makes Sebastian His own child. Through the waters of Baptism, Sebastian gains a new life in Christ Jesus, which helps shape his entire future.

God made Sebastian His own child through the waters of Baptism.

No one would have been surprised that baby Sebastian Bach would grow up to be a musician. Sebastian's ancestors included over twenty musicians. In years to come, Sebastian and his sons and their families would add to that number, so that the Bach family would eventually include seventy-five musicians. The Bach musical dynasty is unmatched in history, even to this day. When all of the Bach cousins, uncles, aunts, and grandparents got together, they made music together. They would even make up funny songs to sing.

Martin Luther was also a musician. He sang in the choir, played the **viol,** and wrote many songs. Luther even said that next to the Bible, music is the most important gift God gave us. Sebastian's destiny would be closely tied with the work of the great reformer. As an adult, Sebastian had many books. Because he wanted to write music to the glory of God, Sebastian often studied theology and the teachings of the Lutheran Church. Much of his large personal library was made up of books written by Martin Luther.

Sebastian's father, Ambrosius, taught him to play the violin.

◆ ◆ ◆

chapter two
Sebastian's Childhood

When he turned eight years old, Sebastian's parents sent him to the same grade school in Eisenach that Martin Luther had attended. Those early days in school were happy ones! Young Sebastian started to read. He learned arithmetic, studied the Bible and the catechism, and played during recess. And he loved to make music with his classmates. At home, his father, Ambrosius, taught him how to play the violin.

But the good times did not last long. Two tragedies struck while Sebastian was still quite young. When he was nine years old, his mother died. Then the next year, while he was still feeling sad and missing his mother, his father passed away too. Losing his mother and father while so young affected Sebastian throughout his life. He would make sure his own family felt loved and cared for.

After his parents died, Sebastian went to live with his older brother, 24-year-old Johann Christoph, who already cared for a young family of his own. They lived in the city of Ohrdruf, not far from Eisenach.

Johann Christoph Bach was also a musician (no surprise there!). He taught school and served as organist at St. Michael's Lutheran Church in Ohrdruf. To help provide for his family, Christoph also tuned and repaired organs. Sebastian's older brother treated Sebastian like a son. Christoph even continued the music education Sebastian had begun with their father. He taught Sebastian to play the organ, the **clavichord,** and the **harp-sichord.** Sebastian showed intense interest in music and discovered early that he had a special talent.

Christoph once described some music as too difficult for young Sebastian, and he would not allow his younger brother to practice it. So, for almost six months, Sebastian would get out of bed late at night and sneak into the room where the music was hidden. By moonlight, he slowly made his own copy. Sebastian could not resist the opportunity to learn new music!

His brother had Sebastian help him fix and tune organs. Sebastian continued to use this skill throughout his life, not only to make extra money, but also to help design new organs for churches.

Although Sebastian greatly missed his mom and dad, he enjoyed life in his brother's home. But as time went by, Christoph's family got larger, and soon there was no room for Sebastian. Only five years after his parents' deaths, Sebastian's life was about to change again.

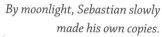

By moonlight, Sebastian slowly made his own copies.

Most nights they slept under the stars.

chapter three
Sebastian
Goes Out on His Own

At age 15, Sebastian decided to go out on his own. On Easter Day in 1700, he sadly said good-bye to his brother's family and set out with his friend Georg Erdmann to travel the 200 miles to the town of Lüneburg. There, Sebastian and Georg would attend St. Michael's School and Monastery to learn more about singing, playing instruments, and even writing music! Along the way as they walked, people sometimes let the boys sleep in their barns. (They may have traveled part of the way by coach.) Most nights, though, they slept outside under the stars. Some folks gave them a few pennies when they sang songs or when Sebastian played his violin.

After many long days, Sebastian and Georg arrived in Lüneburg. At St. Michael's, older boys such as Sebastian could earn a living by singing in their chapel choir as a **chorister**. In return, he was given all his meals, a room with a bed and other furniture, and even pocket money to spend each week as he wanted. He attended lessons at school, and he liked to go to the library to study the music of great composers. Later, he began to play violin in the orchestra. Sebastian made many friends among the monks and the other student singers.

In Lüneburg, Sebastian began to hear the music of many famous composers, not only from Germany but from France and Italy as well. He would often walk to the seaport city of Hamburg, known for its great **opera** performances. On one such trip, Sebastian was hungry but had almost no money. He sat down outside an inn. When a kitchen window opened behind him, two herring heads flew outside, right over his head! Sebastian found a coin in each of these. It was enough to pay for dinner and another trip to Hamburg to hear opera again! Sebastian never found out who gave him these coins, but he knew God was watching over him.

The more music Sebastian heard, the more ideas he had about writing his own songs. Soon he tried his hand at writing music. Some of his early efforts were not very good. But Sebastian kept on trying to get better and better as a composer.

Sebastian never found out who gave him these coins, but he knew God was watching over him.

After a few years, Sebastian felt ready to begin his career as a musician. At age 18, he left St. Michael's Monastery and School to find his own way in the world.

He worked at writing music every day.

chapter four

Sebastian's Early Career

The year 1703 was full of opportunities for Sebastian. In March, he began his career as a violinist in the Weimar court. He felt privileged to be a professional musician playing for royalty. Imagine getting paid for what you already love to do! Still, after a few months, Sebastian became tired of this job. In August, he auditioned to be the organist at New Church in Arnstadt. We know that he must have been a very talented organist because the congregation hired him right away. They paid a generous salary for such a young man. People at New Church loved to hear him perform, and they enjoyed singing hymns as he led them. Sebastian was glad they accepted him so well. The people of the church became his new family.

Here, he began to write music for the organ. He worked every day at writing music. Some days, Sebastian found satisfaction in what he wrote. But other days, he did not. He kept trying. And he would listen to music written by other people. From them he would get ideas about how to improve his own pieces. During the four years he stayed at New Church, Sebastian wrote a lot of organ music. Some of the pieces were elaborations of hymns and songs his listeners already knew. But some pieces, often called **preludes** and **fugues**, were completely original, and people found them quite amazing. Still, Bach's greatest music cannot be found among these works.

Sebastian also had the opportunity to play many different pipe organs. During this time, the famous Silbermann brothers built more than seventy big pipe organs. Many of these are still being played today, over 300 years later! The Silbermann brothers built instruments to last a long time. When churches invited Sebastian to try out their new pipe organs, he would make up big, loud pieces on the spot to test the power of the bellows. In those days, people had to pump the bellows (the "lungs" of an organ) by hand, so that air would go into the pipes!

Sebastian always wanted to improve as a composer. So he asked his church if he could have time off to travel to the town of Lübeck, where a famous organist named Dietrich Buxtehude lived and worked. His church said he could be gone for four weeks. After a long walk to Lübeck, Sebastian enjoyed his visit with Buxtehude and learned very much.

But he lost track of the time. Instead of staying four weeks, he stayed four months! His church in Arnstadt was *not* happy! Sebastian continued as organist at New Church a while longer, but tensions had started to build. Sebastian loved to play elaborate music, but the congregation wanted shorter, simpler music in church. He also had to rehearse the very unruly boys choir every week. Eventually, in the summer of 1707, he decided to move to the city of Mühlhausen and become an organist there.

This proved to be a wonderful place for Sebastian to live. In October of that year, he married Maria Barbara, whom he had first met in Arnstadt. While living in Mühlhausen, Sebastian wrote his first **cantata**. A cantata is a long piece of church music—usually about 20 minutes—that is composed for a choir, various soloists, and an orchestra. He called his first cantata "God Is My King." This title is not surprising, for Sebastian clearly loved God. In all he did, he was careful to give God the glory for his talent and work. But even this cantata was not Sebastian's greatest song.

Maria Barbara Bach

Unfortunately, Sebastian found it very expensive to live in Mühlhausen. He did not have enough money to support himself and his wife, Maria, not to mention the children who soon followed. The people at the church liked Sebastian a lot, but just a year earlier, about one-fourth of the town had burned down, and the town's people were busy trying to rebuild. They could not do much to help with Sebastian's financial needs. Once again, Sebastian made a big change in his life. Now his career would really take off!

In 1708, at age 23, Sebastian moved with Maria to Weimar, where he had won a job as musician in the court of Duke Wilhelm Ernst. The duke wanted Sebastian to play the organ, violin, viola, and harpsichord in his court. It was not easy working for nobility!

But Sebastian's music was exactly what the court needed. He made beautiful music for their parties and ceremonies. And the fancier the music was, the more the duke could make other rulers jealous.

Duke Wilhelm was a Lutheran, and he liked hearing the music Sebastian played. He wanted Sebastian to write music for the Church that would give glory to God.

Sebastian enjoyed a good life working in the court. By age 29, he was promoted to **concertmaster**, or leader, of the orchestra and of all the court's music. Now he was expected to write a long cantata

Duke Wilhelm was not happy about this.

each month. Sebastian stayed at the Weimar court until he was 32. Then he decided to move to an even bigger court! Duke Wilhelm was definitely not happy about this. He was so upset that he put Sebastian in jail for a month before letting him leave.

In 1717, Sebastian moved with his wife, Maria Barbara, and their children to Köthen, where Prince Leopold not only served as a ruler but also played in the orchestra. Here, Sebastian had even more freedom to perform and to write music. Sebastian and the young prince became good friends and often traveled together. The six years he spent in Köthen were some of the happiest of his life.

Prince Leopold was a good friend.

He made many friends and enjoyed the respect of his fellow musicians. Best of all, it seemed that music could be heard all around him!

But tragedy struck once more. Sebastian's wife died. In 1721, he married Anna Magdalena, who had a beautiful singing voice. Sometimes, the Bachs played music and sang together at home. Sebastian's life became full and happy, but also very busy. During this time, Sebastian continued to write many pieces of music— some for instruments and some for keyboard. You may have heard some of these pieces before, such as the Brandenburg **Concertos.** These are still famous and loved today and are performed on many occasions. But even these were not Sebastian's greatest songs.

Sebastian enjoyed his life as a court musician and composer, but still he wanted something more. He wanted to return to his first love—making music for the Church.

Sebastian's life became full and happy, but also very busy.

St. Thomas Lutheran Church in Leipzig, Germany

◆ ◆ ◆

chapter five

Sebastian Makes Music in Church and at Home

In 1723, Sebastian auditioned for the job of **cantor** (one who leads a congregation's singing) at St. Thomas Church in Leipzig, a large, important city. Surprisingly, even though he was famous, Sebastian was not the congregation's first choice for a new organist. In fact, neither was he the second choice. Only after the first two applicants bowed out was Sebastian given the job of music director for the city and its four churches.

He also became a teacher in the school and a choir director at the university. One of the town council members said, "Since we cannot get the best, we have to settle for Bach." But soon, Sebastian's music was heard throughout the entire town! Everyone came to love his music.

Sebastian lived in Leipzig for the rest of his life. There were ups and downs, of course. Sebastian got into arguments with both the church officials and the city council. Often, they disagreed about money. Sebastian's family was growing.

Sebastian got into arguments with the church officials and the city council.

In ten years, Sebastian and Anna Magdalena had ten children, and with a big family come big expenses! Sebastian depended on his salary, but he also needed the money he was paid for performing weddings at the church. Some of the wealthy members were rather mean. They would have their weddings at other churches, just so Sebastian would not get the money he needed! Sebastian struggled for their respect and support, and eventually he won them over.

Sebastian also taught in the Lutheran school in Leipzig. At first, he found this hard. The school had become run down and was in bad shape. But Sebastian faithfully taught his classes and music lessons to the students. Eventually, the school hired a new principal, and the situation changed for the better.

During his years in Leipzig, Sebastian wrote a great deal of music. He was expected to write a long **cantata** for every Sunday of the year! These cantatas were based on the Scripture readings for the day. This meant that each week, he composed the music and wrote out by hand all the sheets of music for the singers and instrumentalists. His wife and children often helped him. Today, about two hundred of these cantatas are still performed.

At the school, Sebastian was very busy with his new music. Besides the many cantatas he wrote in Leipzig, Sebastian wrote his most famous keyboard music, the *Goldberg Variations*, for one of his most talented students, Johann Gottlieb Goldberg. In addition, Sebastian wrote

two of his best-known large choral pieces while at Leipzig— *St. Matthew Passion* (over two hours in length) and the *Christmas Oratorio* (which is actually six cantatas linked together). But even these pieces and the many beautiful cantatas were not Sebastian's greatest songs.

The later years in Sebastian's life were among his most productive. His works, written in the popular baroque musical style of the day, were well-received and made him even more famous. Musicians from all over Europe journeyed to Leipzig to visit the great musician and learn from

him. Once, Sebastian received an invitation to visit the palace of King Frederick the Great of Prussia. When he arrived, he found Frederick about to begin a concert in which Frederick himself was going to play the flute with the orchestra. Frederick quickly canceled the concert and invited Sebastian to play. Sebastian asked Frederick to give him a theme on which to improvise. Together, Frederick and Sebastian improvised on the theme with amazing skill. Later, to mark the occasion, Sebastian developed the theme into a larger work titled *A Musical Offering.*

Together, Frederick and Sebastian improvised on the theme with amazing skill.

*The children often ran out
to the countryside to play and have fun.*

Throughout his years of serving as a musician in palaces and churches, Sebastian could also be found writing at home. His second wife, Anna Magdalena, shared his love of music. Because Anna loved flowers and

songbirds, he wrote a book of poems for her called *The Anna Magdalena Notebook*. He wanted his children to love music too. Sometimes, he would write little songs for them to practice (instead of working on boring exercises) so they could have fun while learning to play. The older Bach children often helped the younger ones with their studies. Music gave the many Bach children a way to have fun with their brothers and sisters and with their mom and dad.

During their years in Leipzig, a bridge crossed the moat that surrounded the city, and a path led into the pastures. The children often ran out to the countryside to play and have fun. Because Sebastian remembered his feelings of loneliness when his parents died, he was determined to provide a happy life for his own family.

Not all days passed without trouble and heartache in the Bach family. One of Sebastian's sons, Wilhelm, left home for over a year and got into serious debt. But Sebastian welcomed him back home and forgave him. Later in life, Wilhelm became a famous musician. Johann Christoph, Sebastian's youngest son, also became famous as a musician in his day. In fact, he eventually became the music director for the queen of England! And he had great influence on a young Austrian boy named Wolfgang Amadeus Mozart. But it was Sebastian's son Carl Philip Emmanuel who gained the greatest musical reputation. Even today, he is the most famous Bach (after his father). Carl Philip Emmanuel loved his father and tried to make sure his father's music was passed on to the next generation.

◆ ◆ ◆

chapter six
Sebastian's Greatest Song

In Sebastian's last great effort, he strived to express everything he had learned as a musician and a composer. He called this masterpiece *The Art of the* **Fugue**. It still stands today as an enormous accomplishment. But even this was not Sebastian's greatest song.

Although many people continued to hear and enjoy Sebastian's music, times changed. Even at the end of Sebastian's life, his friends and admirers had to defend his style of music against many critics. With the passing of time, Johann Sebastian Bach's music was forgotten for a while. About a hundred years after Sebastian's death, another famous Lutheran musician, Felix Mendelssohn, discovered Sebastian's music and reintroduced it to the world. From that time on, it remained extraordinarily popular. About 800 of Sebastian's works are still around today (500 are from his church music and 300 from his days in the palaces). Even now, people around the world are excited to hear the wonderful music of this man.

Johann Sebastian Bach

Many people consider Johann Sebastian Bach the greatest composer in history. Singers and instrumentalists of every nation and culture learn and perform his songs. Doctors have even found that listening to his music helps people who are sick, so his music is used in hospitals as therapy. In 1977, the United States launched the space probe Voyager. Onboard the probe are recordings of Bach's music, and Voyager is still making its way into deepest space today. But even this is not Sebastian's greatest achievement.

Singers and instrumentalists of every nation and culture learn and perform Bach's songs.

Although he wrote music for all kinds of situations and people, Sebastian's greatest song—his finest accomplishment—was the life he lived as a loving husband and father, a teacher, a musician, a composer for everyone. Throughout his life, Sebastian remembered his Baptism. He remembered how God had made him His own and blessed him with many things—his family, his talents, his experiences.

But most of all, he remembered God had graced him with his Savior Jesus Christ. That made all the difference in Sebastian's life. He did not focus on *who* he was, but rather on *whose* he was. He was a beloved child of the heavenly Father. During his whole life, Sebastian was busy making God's song his own greatest song.

On July 22, 1750, Sebastian went to Holy Communion in St. Thomas Lutheran Church for the last time. Soon after, he had a stroke and became very sick. He died six days later.

At the end of each of his many pieces of music, Sebastian always wrote the letters **SDG**. Those letters are an abbreviation for "**Soli Deo Gloria**," which is Latin for "To God alone be the glory." But we can also imagine that the letters stood for something else:

Sebastian **D**evoted to **G**od.

God gave Sebastian a strong faith in Jesus. He also gave him outstanding talents to use to praise Him and to serve others.

In the same way, God gives each of us our talents and the desire and ability to develop them and put them into good use as we serve our family, our friends, and others. God's song is in each of us. Our life is our song back to Him. God hears what we sing as the song of His love plays in our life.

All glory be to God in everything we do!

During his whole life, Sebastian was busy making God's song his own greatest song.

Timeline of Events
during Johann S. Bach's Life

1685   Johann Sebastian Bach born
in Eisenach, Germany, on March 21

1692   Witch trials held in Salem, Massachusetts

1695   After his parents' deaths, Sebastian moves
to Ohrdruf to live with his brother

1698   Cotton Mather publishes his story about
Squanto

1700   Sebastian becomes a chorister at
St. Michael's in Lüneburg

1703   At age 18, Sebastian is named court musician
(violinist) in Weimar by Duke Herzog Johann
Ernst; at end of year Sebastian becomes
organist at New Church, Arnstadt

1705   Sebastian visits Buxtehude, an organist
in Lübeck

1707   Sebastian becomes organist at St. Blasius
in Mühlhausen; writes his first cantata,
"God Is My King"; marries Maria Barbara

1708 Sebastian becomes organist in the court of Duke William Ernst in Weimar

1714 Sebastian is promoted to court concert-master and writes much of his organ music.

1717 Sebastian is appointed to court at Köthen, a German provincial capital; where Prince Leopold names him director of chamber music

1720 Sebastian's wife, Maria Barbara, dies; writes a cantata for young Prince Leopold

1721 Sebastian marries Anna Magdalena; writes much of his "happy" music, including the Brandenburg Concertos

1772 Sebastian gives Anna a book of poems and music

1723 Sebastian is appointed cantor at St. Thomas Lutheran Church, Leipzig

1728 Vitus Bering explores the strait that now bears his name

1733 Benjamin Franklin begins publishing *Poor Richard's Almanac*

1736 Sebastian takes on duties at the Dresden court, while keeping his position at St. Thomas

1742 Handel's *Messiah* is performed for the first time

1747 Sebastian composes *A Musical Offering*

1748 "Now I Lay Me Down to Sleep" appears in *New England Primer;* continues work on his final masterpiece, *The Art of the Fugue*

1749 George Washington becomes a land surveyor at age 17

1750 Johann Sebastian Bach dies on July 28 after having a stroke

Glossary

cantata Longer choral piece (usually lasting about 20 minutes) that features sections sung by various soloists and parts by the choir. A cantata is similar to an opera but can be sung in a church service. It is usually accompanied by an orchestra.

cantor Someone who leads the congregation's songs. Usually the organist and choir director.

chorister Singer in a choir.

clavichord Earliest type of stringed keyboard instrument.

concertmaster Leader of the orchestra, usually the first violinist.

concerto Piece of music featuring a solo instrument, accompanied by the rest of the orchestra.

fugue Complex type of musical composition, in which various voices are placed on top of one another, each singing their independent melody. This differs from most music, in which a single melody is accompanied with harmony by the other singers or instrumentalists.

harpsichord Keyboard instrument of the 1500–1700s. Similar to the piano, except that the strings are plucked rather than struck by a hammer.

opera Musical drama where everything is sung, even the dialogue, usually accompanied by an orchestra.

prelude Piece of music played before a church service or ceremony

viol Delicate stringed instrument used in the 1500s; forerunner of the violin.

Map of Germany in Bach's Time

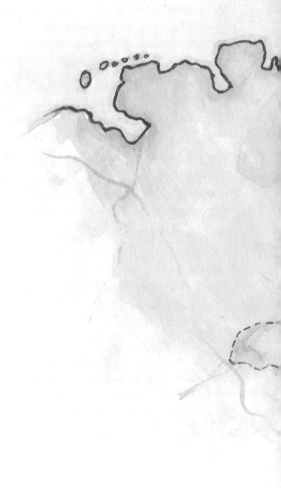

Lübeck

Hamburg

Lüneburg

Köthen

Mühlhausen   Leipzig

Eisenach   Weimar

Ohrdruf

Arnstadt

The Light has returned as it came once before,

the Song of the Lord is our own song once more,

so let us all sing with one heart and one voice

the Song of the Singer in whom we rejoice.

To you, God the Singer, our voices we raise,

to you, Song Incarnate, we give all our praise,

to you, Holy Spirit, our life and our breath,

be glory for ever, through life and through death.

Text: © Peter W. A. Davison, b. 1936. Used with permission.